THE YOUNG GHANAIAN STORY BOOK

The 26 Stories That Depict The Values Of The National Anthem And The Pledge To Ghana In Relation With The Ghanaian Value System

Dipo Toby Alakija

© Copyright 2019 by 'Dipo Toby Alakija

All rights reserved. No part of this book may be reproduced or transmitted in any form or by any means without permission of the publisher.

ISBN: 978-978-8032144
978-8032-1-4-1

Printed in the United States

Published in 2019 by
CALVARY ROCK PUBLISHING

19, Ajina Street, Ikenne Remo,
Ogun State,
Nigeria.

In Conjunction With
CHRISTIAN EDUCATION AND MINISTRATION SERVICES (CEMS)

INTRODUCTION OF THE YOUNG GHANIAN AND OTHER STORY BOOKS BY THE AUTHOR

It has taken more than ten years to package this and other books like The Young Nigerian Story Book, "Foundation And Young Generation Bible Club and other story books, which are in use in many parts of the world, including US and UK. Thus it will take a while to study each of this book which is designed for the purposes of building the National Values through the lessons in the National Anthem and The pledge, embedding either Traditional, Religious or Family Values in the impressionable young minds.

This volume is customized and designed to teach young Ghanians the National Anthem and The Pledge To Ghana and the implications of violating any of rules and regulations that are embedded in them through the use of stories and poems.

Studies and personal experience reveal that children are inclined to grow up with what they are made to believe despite genetic, environmental and other factors. Juveniles on the other hand can easily grow out of hand if they do not get the right answers to vital questions about life. Take for instance, a sixteen year old girl who tried to look for reasons she was alive by writing a letter in a book titled "Between Parents and teenagers" by Dr Haim G. Ginott. The letter says, *"the more I read about life's splendour, the more I see its tragedy: The fleetingness of time, the ugliness of age, the certainty of death. The inevitable is always on my mind. Time is my slow executioner. When I see large crowds at a beach, or a ball game, I think to myself: Who among them is going to die first, and who last? How many of them will be dead next year? Five years from now? Ten years from now? I feel like crying out: How can you enjoy life when you know death is around the corner?"*

This youth is at the dangerous stage of life. The answer she gets to a question like this can influence her to turn to God or drugs or any other things that suggest solutions. The contribution or neglect or answers to questions like this when adults were young made them what they are now. The same things are applicable to this girl. All young ones, whether they know it or not, need the help of godly people to guide them in their stages of life. Although, certain genetic factors may influence young ones just like every other human beings, they are not as effective as the education through what they can perceive with their senses in their environment. Invariably, younger generation is the product of the older one through the environment that is created for them. Juvenile delinquency is often as a result of lack of attention of the adults. Parents have put too much of their future into the hands of other people by neglecting their primary responsibilities to their children. The young ones that are left to parent themselves are often the ones that are organized into vice rings. Instead of building more prisons that will accommodate more criminals who the modern world are breeding through means of entertainments; information and even education, efforts should be made by parents; schools; communities; government; private and public organizations to build the young ones in their countries into responsible citizens through these means. The reason is that a neglected child today is the one that turns into a heartless person who gets involved in crimes, posing serious threat to many lives and even the peace of the nation tomorrow. So parents must see their homes and teachers must consider their schools as places where they breed either criminals or responsible citizens of their countries. In essence, a child can be a curse or a blessings, depending on how he or she is raised up. Many potential leaders of tomorrow are being neglected at the time they needed help most. Some adults are bad influence to many young ones. Their words and attitudes have corrupted their manners.

Young ones at every level need to be disciplined, cultured and tutored about what is expected of them. At that young age, their minds are still very flexible. They are like blank tape that you can record anything you want. Whatever is recorded in their minds is what they would play back to you when they grow older.

This and other books serve the purposes that are indicated in the next page.

In the final analysis, I would like to refer to the old adage that says parents should train their children in the way they want them to go and when they are old, they will not leave the path. Most parents have failed to teach their children family values, leaving them to parent themselves. The result of that is to leave them at the mercy of agents of corruption that now made it possible for a twelve-year old girl to be a mother. Because many school teachers all over the world had been influenced to believe in wrong set of values, they also failed in their responsibilities to the nation by failing to teach their students societal values, some of which are embedded in the national anthem and the pledge to their countries. Again, the result of that is to have young ones getting involved in vices and even crimes.

This book makes attempt to equip teachers and parents with materials that can be used to rebuild the Family Values and the Value System of Ghana through young minds.

I sincerely hope it serves this purpose.

- 'Dipo Toby Alakija

THE PURPOSES AND THE USE OF "THE YOUNG GHANAIAN STORY BOOK" AS SUGGESTED BY THE AUTHOR

It is important to explain the purposes of this book so as to understand how to make best use of it. As indicated in the book titled "The Values Of The National Anthems And The Pledge To Ghana" which is designed by the author for youths and adults, a close study of National Anthems and The Pledge of Ghana will reveal the framework of the Ghanaian Value System. If this framework is neglected, instead of people in positions of influence like parents; teachers; political; community and other leaders to build upon it, there would be chaos, vices and crimes in the organized society. Thus "The Young Ghanian Story Book" is designed to teach and embed in young minds the values of the National Anthem and The Pledge To Ghana in relation to the value system through stories and poems. It attempts to interpret the meanings of the anthem and the pledge, boosting their moral values and giving them the picture of what the law says.

The book contains 26 stories, each of which is titled with a line or lines of the National Anthem and The Pledge to Ghana. The stories are as follow:

THE FIRST STANZA OF THE NATIONAL ANTHEM
Story 1 In Page 9: God Bless Our Homeland, Ghana
 And Make Our Nation Great And Strong,
Story 2 In Page 11: Bold To Defend Forever
 The Cause Of Freedom And Of Right;
Story 3 In Page 13: Fill Our Hearts With True Humanity,
 Make Us Cherish Fearless Honesty,
Story 4 In Page 15: And Help Us Resist Oppressor's Rule
 With All Our Will And Might For Evermore

THE SECOND STANZA OF THE NATIONAL ANTHEM
Story 5 In Page 17: Hail To Thy Name, O Ghana
 To Thee We Make Our Solemn Vow;
 Steadfast To Build Together
Story 6 In Page 19: A Nation Strong In Unity;
 With Our Gifts Of Mind And Strength Of Arm,
Story 7 In Page 21: Whether Night And Day, In Midst Of Storm,
Story 8 In Page 23: In Every Need, Whate'ver The Call May Be,
 To Serve Thee, Ghana, Now And Evermore

THE THIRD STANZA OF THE NATIONAL ANTHEM

Story 9 In Page 25: Raise High The Flag Of Ghana
                              And One With Africa Advance;
Story 10 In Page 27: Black Star Of Hope And Honour
                              To All Who Thirst For Liberty;
Story 11 In Page 29: Where The Banner Of Ghana Freely Flies,
Story 12 In Page 31: May The Way To Freedom Truly Lie;
Story 13 In Page 33: Arise, Arise, O Sons Of Ghana Land
                              And Under God March On For Evermore!

THE PLEDGE TO GHANA

Story 14 In Page 35: I Promise, On My Honour
Story 15 In Page 37: To Be Faithful
Story 16 In Page 39: And Loyal To Ghana
Story 17 In Page 41: My Motherland
Story 18 In Page 43: I Pledge Myself
Story 19 In Page 45: To Service Of Ghana
Story 20 In Page 47: With all My Strength
                              And With All My Heart
Story 21 In Page 49: I Promise To Hold In High Esteem
                              Our Heritage Won For Us
Story 22 In Page 51: Through The Blood and Toil Of Our Fathers
Story 23 In Page 53: And I Pledge Myself In All Things
Story 24 In Page 55: To Uphold And Defend
Story 25 In Page 57: The Good Name Of Ghana
Story 26 In Page 59: So Help Me God

SERIES OF WEEKLY GHANIAN CHILDREN AND YOUTH ORIENTATION STUDIES

1st Series Of Studies In Page 61
2nd Series Of Studies In Page 62
3rd Series Of Studies In Page 63
4th Series Of Studies In Page 64
5th Series Of Studies In Page 65

The book can be studied for more than a session either as a Junior Literary Work materials or Civics or Moral Instruction or other textbooks. This largely depends on the field or skill or creativity of the teacher. As a guide, the followings are the ways the use of the book can be maximized.

ACADEMIC PURPOSE

Since the book introduces civic responsibilities to young minds, it gives them the picture of the Ghanaian Value System and makes them understand that breaking any of the pledges they make to the nation can lead to breaking the law. It also serves as materia that teach them law, order and the implications of violating them. Apart from this, it recalls a few historical and other facts in the way young minds can comprehend them and appreciate the sacrifices of Ghanaian fallen heroes.

LITERARY PURPOSE

The stories and poems are treated in ways that will capture the imaginations of young minds with facts and realities as distinguished from imaginary stories which most children are familiar with. The poems which are to be memorized with the aim of embedding values are also designed to inspire them to be imaginative and creative. Students are encouraged to compose the poems into songs, which can inspire creativity.

PURPOSE OF MORAL INSTRUCTIONS

All the stories are narrated with the aim of teaching one moral lesson or the other. Results of research works reveal that if children are impacted with the belief in God as both the anthem and the pledge indicate, they would be God-fearing as they grow up. God-fearing people are law-abiding people.

OTHER USEFUL PURPOSES

The book can be used to engaged students in extra curricular activities like using the stories they have studied to present dramas, using the poems to compose songs or debating and comparing the activities of characters like mice; menaces and Compatriots in relation to present day events. They can also be made to write their own stories or essays, which may reveal how much they have been impacted.

The students will be impacted if the book is used for the above purposes.

STORY ONE

God Bless Our Homeland Ghana And Make Our Nation Great And Strong,

The coast in West Africa called Ghana is blessed with gold, gifted and Godly people who make the nation great and strong. Shortly after independence, the citizens were ready to use what God has given them, including natural resources and gifts of mind to bake the cake that would be big enough for both old and young people to eat. When it was baked, it was so big that there were lots of leftovers for children who were yet unborn after the people have taken their fair share.

Mice soon found their ways to where the people were baking the cake and began to eat it. They also destroy the things that are used to bake it, teaching their children how to eat and destroy them by making them watch the way they did it. This began to cause lots of problems like shortage of food and money for a very long time. Many people, including children who were once good started looking for food and money by all means. Many people began to steal and even kill one another for money or food.

Later, some compatriots cried out to other citizens who are suffering, "let us pray to God to help us drive away the mice that are eating and destroying our cake." They begin to gather everywhere, including schools and pray everyday, saying, "God bless our homeland Ghana and make our nation great and strong!" God answered them by giving them four heroes who will help them chase the mice away. The persons are called Unity Of the people, Gifts Of Mind, Strength Of Arms and Fearless Honesty.

Through these persons, the citizens are able to drive away the mice. The citizens begin to bake the cake again.

CAT AND RAT

There is a rat in the room
Sweeping around like broom
Martins hears and sees the rat
It seems so smart and so fat
That he feels it like a loom
He goes out of the room
And calls outside at the cat
Shouting, "chase that cat!"
The cat chase the rat with a zoom
Until it goes into its doom!

Class Activities

1. Teacher: Explain to students that Compatriots are citizens who do right things and mice are those who do wrong.
2. Ask them of the wrong and right things they notice around them.
3. Ask them what they can do to stop wrong things from happening.
4. Make them understand how wrong things can affect them in future.
5. Make them memorize the poem or compose it into a song.

STORY TWO
Bold To Defend Forever
The Cause Of Freedom And Of Right;

A snake went to a chicken that was brooding over its little ones. The snake made lots of hissing sounds and expected the chicken to flee. The snake wanted to grab all the little ones and swallow them as food. The chicken refused to leave its little ones. The snake struck it several times with its venom until the chicken died right on top of its little ones, using its body to protect them.

When it could not get the little ones, the snake went away.

The following day, the owner of the chicken went to the barn to feed it. Through its wounds, he knew a snake must have struck it dead and thought the little ones must be dead too. When he removed the dead chicken, he saw that the little ones were alive and healthy. He was so moved by what the chicken did that he decided that he would not let its sacrifice to be in vain by protecting all its little ones until they grow into big chicken.

All young Ghanians must see themselves as the little ones while the chicken represent all the Compatriots who have sacrificed many things, including their lives to protect others from dangers. Snakes are the enemies of the citizens like kidnappers and other menaces who do bad things to other people. The owner of the chicken is the Government.

There are many snakes that are making life difficult for people in Ghana. While the Government tries to protect the people from the snakes, the little ones must not let the sacrifice of the Compatriots to

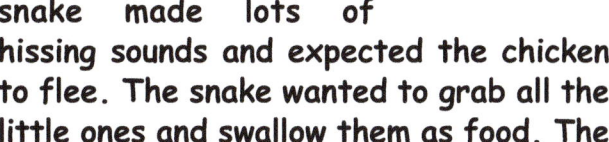

be in vain by giving room for the snakes to attack them. As they grow up, they must "be bold to defend forever the cause of freedom and of right" just like the Compatriots who sacrificed so many things, including their lives while fighting for the rights of the citizens or while defending the nation.

Poem: No Sacrifice, No Hope
If there is no one to plant
There would be no harvest
If people make no sacrifices
There would be no blessings
If there is no sacrifices for all
There is no hope for anyone
If all parents make sacrifices
For the good of their children
The nation would be blessed

Class Activities

1. Teacher: Find hard words in story one and two and tell them to get what they mean.
2. Ask them what they learnt in the story about the chicken and compare it with sacrifices of the nationalists before the independence.
3. Tell them to list all the types of people that can be called snakes.
4. Tell them to memorize the poem or compose it into a song.

STORY THREE
Fill Our Hearts With True Humanity, Make Us Cherish Fearless Honesty,

There was a time in Ghana when there was wealth which brought good health, prosperity, joy, peace and unity among the people. Suddenly, diseases broke out; making the people sick, poor, sad, troubled and divided. Many people, especially young ones began to die one after the other. You know, if there are no longer children, it would get to a time when the country would no longer exist.

Some Compatriots whose hearts are filled with true humanity and fearless honesty rose up to serve their motherland by looking for ways to remove the diseases. They found out that one of the main causes of the diseases was rat poison which the people, especially young ones were fond of taking like fruit drinks. The rat poison which always tasted so sweet was actually meant to kill them slowly.

Now Compatriots have lots of problems to solve. First they have to make the people believe that what tasted like fruit drink was actually rat poison. Secondly, they have to start preparing real fruit drinks that would replace the rat poison. Well, preparing the real fruit drinks was not as difficult as making the people believe that the rat poison was not fruit drink!

This story is actually talking about what is happening in Ghana. The wealth of the nation are things that give people good health; prosperity; joy; peace and unity; which include good leadership and stable economy. The

diseases are misbehaviours of some citizens, including children and their leaders while the rat poison that tastes like fruit drinks includes bad books, dirty television programs, foul films and music that are entertaining but teaching the people wrong things. If people learn wrong things, they will misbehave and become criminals who may be killed or taken to prisons.

Poem: Rat Poison

If you really love Ghana
You will never get the idea
Of giving people rat poison
Which can land them in prison
There are lots of bacteria
That roam around Ghana
This can lead to crime of treason
Which is a gateway to prison

Class Activities

1. Teacher: Explain to the students in details how things they read, see or hear can make them to be well-mannered or to misbehave. Tell them to list and express their views about wrong conduct of people around them.
2. Ask them other things that can be considered as rat poison.
3. Tell them to memorize the poem or compose it into a song.

STORY FOUR

And Help Us Resist Oppressor's Rule With All Our Will And Might For Evermore

There was a king called Justice who used the staff of office called Truth to rule in Gold Coast. Since Justice reigned with the use of Truth, which always revealed secrets of menaces to him, he was able to get Compatriots like Courage, Honesty, Strength, Freedom, Humanity and a host of others to rule with him.

One day, a menace called Deception wanted to rule Gold Coat so as to eat up the cake, which the people have laboured to bake for everybody, including unborn children. He planned with other menaces like Dishonesty, Lies, Fraud and others to steal Truth from the Palace. When they were able to steal the staff through Coup D'etat, they removed Justice with his cabinet of Compatriots from office and began to rule over Gold Coast.

The people soon discovered that Truth had been taken away from the palace. With the missing Truth and the reign of Deception, the people began to suffer from much pains, sorrows, hunger, horror and even loss of lives during this period.

Everybody started crying, asking Justice to come back and rule Gold Coast. Justice was nowhere to be found since the reign of Deception. They went to the few Compatriots around and told them to do something about Menaces, saying, "if you don't bring Justice back to Palace, Menaces will eat the cake in our motherland and starve us and our children to death."

The Compatriots knew they were right. So they gathered in one place and prayed to God to help them resist the oppressor's rule in their homeland.

The compatriots and the people later searched for Justice

and found him alone in a place called Neglected while his cabinet members were found in a place called Rejected.

All the Compatriots led the people to Palace and make the place difficult for menaces to stay. The people were able to take over the palace with the use of Truth and put Justice back on the throne as the king.

POEM: WHEN TRUTH IS MISSING

Wherever truth is missing
Justice can never reign
When Justice does not reign
Criminals become the leaders
Whenever a criminal is a leader
Crimes are the order of the day
Because Crimes are deadly enemies
The people must always look for truth!

Class Activities

1. Teacher: First explain the meanings of the story and the poem in relation to what happened in Ghana during coup d'etat.
2. Tell them to recall the titles in Story One to Four and sing them as the first stanza of the anthem.
2. Explain hard words in story 3 and 4.
3. Tell them to memorize the poem or compose it into a song.

STORY FIVE
Hail To Thy Name, O Ghana To Thee We Make Our Solemn Vow; Steadfast To Build Together

The Gold Coast in West Africa is a beautiful mansion where different groups of people of the same family live. The mansion which was built by God is so gigantic that it can accommodate tens and even hundreds of millions of people at the same time. There are many precious things inside the mansion, which the people can use to get all the things they and their children need in life without problem, suffering and without feeling hungry.

One day, the groups of people began to fight over the precious things in the house. All of them think of how to get as many precious things as they can for themselves instead of thinking of how to trade and increase them. While fighting one another, fire suddenly burst out in the mansion! It began to destroy many lives and the properties in the place. Children, youths and adults began to suffer from the fire.

Some Compatriots like Humanity, Honesty, Freedom, Courage, Peace, Unity and others hear the S.O.S (Save Our Souls) call of fellow citizens to fulfill their solemn vow to build the mansion together. They gathered to talk about saving the people and the mansion from getting ravaged.

As always, the Compatriots first sing the first stanza of the anthem, praying, "God bless our homeland, Ghana and make our nation great and strong, Bold to defend forever the cause of freedom and of right, Fill our hearts with true humanity and help us resist oppressor's rule with all our will and might for evermore!" Then they began to use everything God has given them, including gifts of mind to put off the fire.

Of course, this story is talking about Ghana as a big and beautiful mansion. The groups of people who are of the same family are different tribes that are in the country. The precious things in the house are the natural and other resources in Ghana. The fire is the problems like crimes, lack of food and money.

POEM: STEADFAST TO BUILD

Oh, God who created all things
We call on You to help us to build
And save our nation that is ravaged
By menaces in our motherland
Give us the hearts of love and mercy
And teach us to be of help to others
Help us to use the gifts of mind
To care for all and one another
Give us the strength to overcome
All the menaces that plague the land

Class Activities

1. Teacher: Ask of the opinions of the students about problems in Ghana in relation with the story and ask them how they can put things right.
2. Find hard words in the story and in the poem and explain them.
3. Explain that the poem as a prayer for the nation and tell them to memorize or compose it into a song.

STORY SIX
A Nation Strong In Unity; With Our Gifts Of Mind And Strength Of Arm

There were four young Compatriots who came from the Eastern, Western, Northern and other regions of Ghana. They all wanted to serve their motherland with all their strengths and gifts of mind in building the nation. These services include going from one place to another, teaching the people about building the nation through the use of their talents and strengths.

One of the Compatriots called Lame did not have legs to walk but he has the brain to plan how to build the nation. Another one called Blind could not see but he knew how to talk to people and make them build the nation. Another one called Dumb could not talk with his mouth but he has very strong body. Another one called Stone Deaf could not hear at all but he has sharp eyes that could see when danger was coming to the Compatriots.

Lame began to plan how they would start moving. He told Dumb to carry him on his shoulder and told Blind who was going to talk with the people to hold one of Dumb's hands. He made Deaf to lead them and watch out for danger that might stop them in their services to build the nation. Whenever they came across any menace, the Compatriots would combine their strengths and gifts and fight him until they defeated him.

With time, they were able to gather the people. Blind was made to talk with them about Lame's plan on how to build the nation. He was able to persuade them to join the group. Before long, everybody except the mice and menaces began to build the nation; including baking the national cake.

This story talks about different people in Ghana. Each person has gifts that may be different from others. A person who is not so brilliant may be gifted in sports that can bring pride to Ghana. Another person who is not be good in science subjects which can make him a doctor or an engineer or nurse may be good in art subjects that can make him a good teacher or writer or lawyer. Others who are not able to get higher education can become good business people or industrialists or other experts.

What is important to note in the story is that if you use your gifts for the good of other people, God will bless you through them.

POEM: SERVICE WITH STRENGTH

The founding fathers of Ghana
Taught us to believe and serve God
And To serve God with all my strength
Is to give my heart to God of all
To serve Ghana with gifts of mind
Is to serve the people with my talent
Come what may on our way
God will bless our homeland
Because of our faith in Him
Through our prayers and deeds
God will make our nation great
And we shall be strong again

Class Activities

1. Teacher: Ask the students the lessons in the story.
2. Ask them how they can use their gifts to serve the nation.
3. Make them memorize the poem or compose it into a song.

STORY SEVEN

Whether Night And Day, In Midst Of Storm,

Once upon a time, some Compatriots from every region of Ghana called Faith in God, Love Of Fellow Citizens, Peace, Liberty Of Nation, Unity Of Citizens, Gifts Of Mind, Strength Of People and others went on a biking competition. The first person to complete the race would get gold medal, the second would get silver and the third would get bronze.

Before that day, the Compatriots have prepared very hard so as to make the region they represented proud. Of course, the citizens in all each region were watching the competition, praying to God to make their region to take the gold or silver or bronze medal.

As soon as they were commanded to take off, all the Compatriots began the race. The crowd that was watching them through network of televisions began to cheer the people. Love was taking the lead, followed by Faith, Unity, Peace, Liberty and the rest. Suddenly, the handle of Peace' bicycle loosened and twisted. He lost control of the bicycle and had an accident. He cried out with pains as his body was dragged on the road.

When the rest heard his cries, they were disturbed. Love who was still taking the lead was the first to stop because he knew he must not leave his brother and friend behind and go after the gold as the crowd expected.

The rest of the Compatriots cried at him, 'why do you stop the race?'

Love replied, 'my brother is more important to me than the gold. You can go ahead and get the gold. I am going to help my brother.'

The rest of the Compatriots were moved by Love's action. They also stopped the race and went to help their brother on his feet. They all knew that he would have done the same for them if they were in his shoe. No one won the official gold or silver or bronze medals because no one completed the race but they all won the hearts of the crowd who gave them much more gold.

POEM: LOVE OF THE PEOPLE
My love for fellow Ghanaians
Is my love for my country
He who loves his country
Will make sacrifices for her
The call to serve the citizens
Whatever the call may be
Is the call to serve the nation
I will serve Ghana with my gift

Class Activities

1. Teacher: Compare the attitudes of the compatriots in the story with those who love money more than welfare of other citizens.
2. Ask them what they learned.
3. Explain the lessons in the poem and the story as helping those in need is the best way to serve Ghana.
4. Tell them to memorize the poem or compose it into a song.

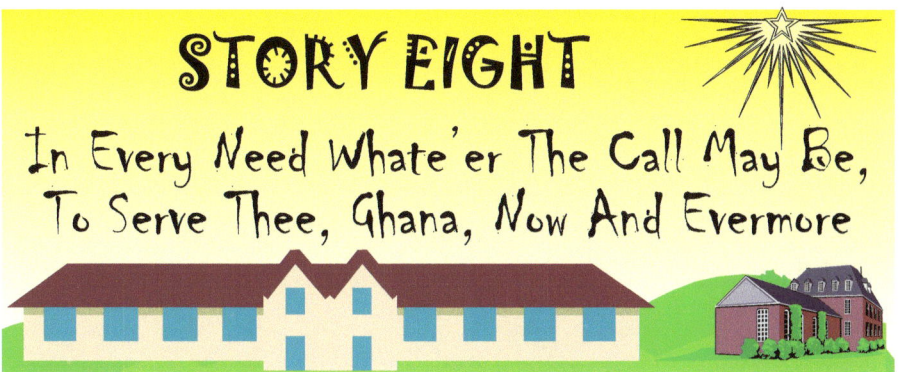

STORY EIGHT
In Every Need Whate'er The Call May Be, To Serve Thee, Ghana, Now And Evermore

During world war II, it was the custom in the United States for families whose sons were serving in the military to place stars in the front windows of their homes. A gold star, however, means that the son had died in support of his country.

There was a man who was walking down the street of New York City with his 5 year old son at this period. The boy asked his father about the stars at the windows of some houses. His father said to him, "the stars are signs that the families in the houses have their sons or daughters serving the nation in the wars." The boy would clap and cheer each of the families wherever he saw the stars after he discovered that their sons or daughters were serving the nation in the night and day in every need.

When they came to an empty space which put a gap between the houses, he looked at the sky and caught his breath. There was a star in the sky. He cried excitedly to his father, "look at the star at the windows of heaven, daddy! God must have given His Son too!"

The boy was just right because the Bible says in John 3:16, "For God so loved the world, that he gave his only begotten Son, that whosoever believes in him should not perish, but have everlasting life."

When people realize what God has sacrificed for them so that they do not go to hell, a place that burns with fire and brimstone, they will use their lives to please Him. If Ghanians also know what the founding fathers has sacrificed for the good of Ghana, they will abide by the law and fulfil the promises they make to the nation. If they use their lives to displease God, they make His sacrifice of no value to them and then walk on the path of hell. If also citizens refuse to fulfil the pledges they make to Ghana, they make the sacrifices of founding fathers useless. The result would be to go into many wars, including wars against vices, crimes and terrorism.

Soldiers And Enemies

Every citizen of Ghana is a soldier
That fights for the good of Ghana Or
An enemy that fights against citizens
By doing good to citizens in need
You are building the nation
If you do or incite others to do wrong
You are the oppressor in the nation

Class Activities

1. Teacher: Use the lessons in the poem and in the story to explain to students ways they can be of help in day and night and in the midst of storm and in every need.
2. Explain the wrong things that can make citizens enemies of Ghana.
3. Tell them to memorize the poem or compose it into a song.

STORY NINE

Raise High The Flag Of Ghana And One With Africa Advance;

One day, an army general decided to move round the city in his parade van with the best of his soldiers after a major victory over the enemies. This was announced to his soldiers in the city and they got ready for the military parade where the general would pick his choice.

All the soldiers except those who were wounded during the advance in the battles against the enemies were present for the parade.

The soldiers were all smartly dressed, armed with their bogus weapons and other military gadgets. Just as the show was getting very interesting, a wounded soldier who felt he was the best left the hospital where he was receiving treatments and made his way to the place with a walking stick and blood stained cloths. His head that was full of wounds was bandaged.

The general saw him afar and asked what he was looking for.

He told him he has come to contest as the best soldier. Most of the soldiers laughed at him but when he told them what he went through in the hands of the enemies while he was trying to defend the country, they knew he really raised the flag of his country high above other soldiers. So he deserved the title of the best soldier. The proofs of his service as a great soldier were all written in wounds.

He was made to ride with the general.

The lives of Compatriots who "raise high the flag of Ghana" are very much like the soldier who risked his life and sacrificed so much to get victory over the enemies or to get independence from the colonial masters. Such Compatriots include Dr Kwame Nkrumah who was one of those who fought for the freedom of Ghana and that of other African countries. Other Ghanian heroes include Dr John Kofi, Agyekun Kufuor, Joseph Boakye Danquah, Ebenezer Ako-

Adjei, Edward Akufo-Addo, William Ofori Atta, Ebenezar Ako-Adjei, Emmanuel Obetsebi-Lamptey and so many others whose names are found in the history of Ghana.

> **Poem: Sacrifice For Ghana**
> If you are truly a Compatriot
> You will sacrifice for Ghana
> I am a Ghanaian Compatriot
> I will make sacrifices for Ghana
> By loving other Ghanaians
> It does not matter where they are
> I will care for them like a family
> Help me to care for them, oh God!

Class Activities

1. Teacher: Use the poem to explain to students ways they can prove that they love Ghana.
3. Ask them of other ways they can raise high the flag of Ghana..
2. Further explain the things that can be considered wars in the society and ask them what they learn in the lessons.
3. Tell them to memorize the poem or compose it into a song.

STORY TEN
Black Star Of Hope And Honour To All Who Thirst For Liberty;

Abraham Lincoln was an American lawyer and politicians who was born in 1809. He served as the 16th President of the United States at the period of slavery until he was killed in 1861 for doing the right thing. Civil war broke out during his government, which brought about the end of slavery in American.

Before this time, Abraham Lincoln once watched a plantation owner trying to buy a black slave girl whom he suspected was going to be abused.

Lincoln paid the price and set the slave girl free.

After she had been set free, the slave asked him, "does that mean I can say wherever I want to say?"

He replied, "yes."

"I can go wherever I like?"

Again he replied, "yes."

With tears running down her face, she said, "then, I'll go with you."

Of course, Abraham took her home and took good care of her instead of using her like a slave. In return, the girl obeyed all his instructions.

Ghanaians just like the slave girl were once servants of the Colonial Masters before the independence day on 6th March 1957. After independence day, Ghana became free from colonial rule. Again, just like the slave girl who subjected her freedom to Abraham Lincoln, Ghanaians have to thirst for liberty by following the law of their motherland. This means that just because Ghana is free from colonial rule does not mean the citizens are free to misbehave. Ghanaians can be black stars of hope and honour who all thirst for liberty only if they keep the law and avoid doing wrong things like stealing or cheating during examination. Breaking the law is dishonourable ways of life that take people to prison, where they would lose their freedom or liberty.

POEM: FREEDOM IS A CHOICE

Many people are free by choice
Because they follow the law
Many are in prisons by choice
Because they break the law
Many people will never be free
Because they decide to be slaves
The Slaves of crimes or vices

Class Activities

1. Teacher: Ask the students all they learned in the story about the slave girl and Abraham Lincoln.
2. Explain the poem. Ask them things people do that take them to prisons.
3. Find hard words in story 6-10 and explain them.
4. Tell them to memorize the poem.

STORY ELEVEN
Where The Banner Of Ghana Freely Flies,

Now Dove who was brought up in the right way of life and Vulture who learns wrong things through movies and music are two different birds in Ghana. They have different characters and ways of life. Vulture feels free to do whatever he likes and he eats anything that tastes like food, including rotten meat. (Read again story three about rat poison.)

Dove is taught about flying the banner of Ghana through good behaviour which can make his parents at home and teachers in school proud of him. He also learns to take only what is given to him as a young citizen.

Vulture wants to change Dove's ways of life. So he first makes friends with him. They would have made good friends if they were not different from each other through what they learn from different places.

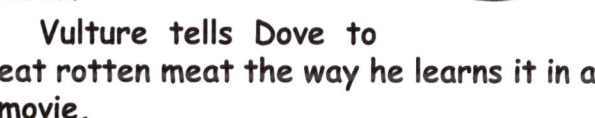

Vulture tells Dove to eat rotten meat the way he learns it in a movie.

Making faces, Dove says, "I'm not taught to eat rotten meat where I come from. My parents said it may kill me if I eat anything like that."

'Don't be a Mama's pet! Everybody eats it. Come on, let's go over there and try it,' Vulture says. 'I've eaten it many times. It is very delicious.'

Dove picked the rotten meat and tries to eat it. It smells horrible! He knows he is not supposed to eat things like that. It will trouble his stomach.

'Come on, eat it up,' Vulture persuades him. 'Watch me...' He picks part of the meat and eats it. 'Yummy! I love it. Come on, try it...'

Dove tries again. Still making faces, he puts it in his mouth... Hmmm ... Raw rotten meat! Disgusting! He says to himself, 'oh, I must not make Vulture feel disappointed.' He swallows it. 'Ooh, terrible taste!'

'Delicious, isn't it?' asks Vulture.

The dove says, 'it is good.' But it is not good for his stomach because the meat cannot digest. It is kept rotten inside his stomach for a long time and causes him much pains until he dies few days later.

This story is about a child who is well brought up at home and taught in school the way he should behave so that he or she can make Ghana proud. But when he makes friends with Vulture by joining bad gang who does thing to be ashamed of such as lying; stealing; fighting and cheating during examination, he too begins to do wrong things. As grows up, he could not do things people can be proud of. Instead, he causes trouble every time. This causes him to go to jail or die young. To fly the banner of Ghana freely is to do things the nation would be proud of. So you must learn to do right thing.

POEM: LITTLE DOVE OF GHANA

Little dove of Ghana is given a banner
Which is the good legacy of Ghana
He flies freely as he grows into adult
His deeds make the nation proud
Before he grows old to fly the banner
He looks for another to give the banner
He sees little one in a house in Ghana
And teach him how to fly the banner

Class Activities

1. Teacher: Explain the above story along with story 3 and then ask the students what they learned.
2. Explain the poem and tell them memorize or compose it into a song.

STORY TWELVE
May The Way To Freedom Truly Lie;

There were two boys called Honesty and Dishonesty who went to the same school. As school children, they were always taught that the true way to freedom is to follow the rules and regulations. During Moral Instructions Class, the teacher would tell them that if they break the rules and regulations as they grow up, they would lose their freedom by going to jail. He also told them, "if you want to be great and successful in life, you must study your books and fulfil all the promises you make to Ghana."

Honesty tried very hard to study his books and fulfil the promises but he could not understand many things that were taught in the class. So he failed during the examinations. Dishonesty who did not read his book at all managed to pass because he cheated during the examination. He was promoted to the next class while Honesty was made to repeat the class.

Honesty cried and said to himself, "I should have cheated too so that I can get promoted like Dishonesty" but the teacher who gave them Moral Instructions encouraged him. He said, "if you don't repeat the class, you will not know what you are supposed to know before you move to the next class. If you study your books well, you will pass and get promoted. The reason you come to school is to learn, not just to pass the examinations."

Honesty was encouraged. He studied and worked very hard to get promoted and become successful while Dishonesty continued to cheat during the examinations. Some years later,

Honesty graduated from the University and became a Lawyer. He later became a Judge.

Dishonesty who never stopped cheating grew into a menace called Fraud. He always looked for quick and easy ways to make money.

One day, the police arrested Dishonesty for using tricks to steal money from a company. He was charged before the court. Do you know who the Judge was? You are right if you say it was Honesty.

Honesty judged and sentenced Dishonesty to prison according to what the law says even though they were once classmates.

POEM: THE PROMISE TO GHANA
The promise to Ghana is good for us
Because it makes us very successful
The promise to Ghana is better for us
Because it makes us very responsible
The promise to Ghana is best for us
Because it makes us march under God

Class Activities

1. Teacher: Ask the students what they learned in the story.
2. Ask them of their opinions about the Judge who sentenced his classmate to prison.
3. Tell them to memorize the poem or compose it into a song.

THE GOD OF CREATION

There was a man known as Atheist
He neither believed there is God
Nor believed the world was created
He planted some seeds on his farm
Rain and sun caused them to grow
When it was time for the harvest
Thieves came and took everything
Atheist cried out, "Oh, my God!"

Class Activities

1. Teacher: ask students to list things made by God and ones made by man.
2. Tell them to write a story or an essay about the foolishness about the person who does not believe there is God.
3. Tell them to memorize the poem or compose it into a song.

STORY FOURTEEN
I Promise, On My Honour

There are some children who are born in different parts of Gold Coast called Ghana. They attend different private and Government schools but they are all made to make the same promise to their motherland, saying, "I promise on my honour..."

Through the national anthem, everybody is made to believe in God who bears witness as they make these promises. God decides to bless anyone who fulfil his or her promises and punish anyone who dares to break them.

As time goes by, some of these children begin to grow into Compatriots like Obedience, Love, Strength, Honesty, Courage, Peace and Liberty who will become leaders in different walks of life as in law, management, civil service, engineering, medicines, education, politics, security and others.

Many other children begin to grow into menaces like Lies, Examination Malpractice, Deceptions, Dishonesty and Frauds that give births to vices that cause people to suffer or crimes that make others to lose their lives.

As years rolls by, the young Compatriots grow into great leaders like honest business people that help others who are in need, good lawyers who helped to get poor but innocent people out of legal problems, responsible political leaders, good teachers who impacted knowledge into others and other successful people whom God uses to make Ghana great and strong.

The children who do not fulfill their promises grow into menaces that grieve their motherland because they do not fulfill their promises. Because of this, God who leads the nation for evermore begins to punish them for the wrongs things they do. Some of them are infected with diseases that cause them to suffer. Some are killed while fighting the Police and some are taken to prisons where they will not see their loved ones.

While Compatriots are full of joy and blessings of God who rewards them for fulfilling their promises, the menaces are full of pains and sorrows.

As a young Ghanaian, you must understand that God gives the people their rewards, according to their works. This is what it really means when you say: "under God match on for evermore!"

POEM: THE PROMISE TO GHANA
The promise to Ghana is good for us
Because it makes us very successful
The promise to Ghana is better for us
Because it makes us very responsible
The promise to Ghana is best for us
Because it makes us march under God

Class Activities

1. Teacher: Explain to the students how breaking the promises to Ghana is breaking the law.
2. Ask them what they learnt in the story.
3. Find hard words in Story 11 to 14 and explain them. Tell them how the pledge can make them responsible.
4. Tell them to memorize the poem or compose it into a song.

STORY FIFTEEN
To Be Faithful

The coast in West Africa called Ghana is so blessed with gold, gifted and Godly people that other countries envied them. Because the people feared God, God made the nation great and strong. There was peace, love and joy after God gave them independence from the British on 6th March 1957. On 24th February 1966, however, some menace called Unfaithful, Disloyal, Dishonest, Oppressor and other unwanted soldiers who felt they should rule Ghana by force took over the Government through what is called Coup d'etat and drove away the people who fought for the independence. There was usually lack of money as the menaces continued to take power and rule. Each time there is problem in the country, some Compatriots like Faithful, Loyal, Honest, Patriotism and Courage would sacrifice many things, trying to bring solution. Menaces who cause the problem in the country always enjoy while the citizens suffer. For this reason a man called Thurgood Marshall said, "Where you see wrong or inequality or injustice, speak out, because this is your country. This is your democracy. Make it. Protect it. Pass it on."

Because you are still young, you may not be able to do anything about this problem but as great Compatriots in the making, you must always talk to God through the use of the prayers in the National Anthem that says, "God Bless Our Homeland Ghana And Make Our Nation Great And Strong, Bold To Defend Forever The Cause Of Freedom And Of Right; Fill Our Hearts With True Humanity, Make Us Cherish Fearless Honesty, And Help Us Resist Oppressor's Rule With All Our Will And Might For Evermore."

As you sing the Anthem always, you will grow up to become

great Compatriots who are fearless, honest, faithful, loyal and powerful enough to put an end to all the activities of the menaces in the society. Then your names will go into the history of Ghana as great Compatriots!

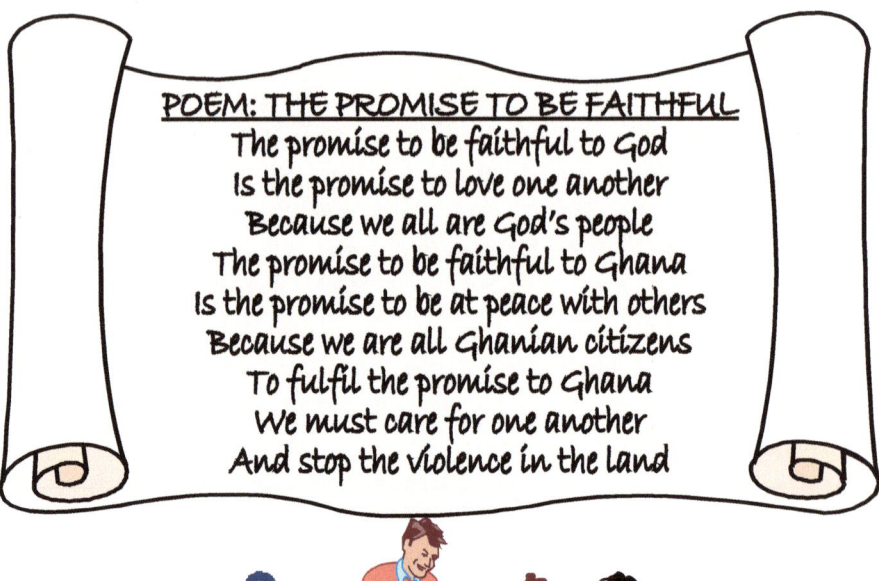

POEM: THE PROMISE TO BE FAITHFUL
The promise to be faithful to God
Is the promise to love one another
Because we all are God's people
The promise to be faithful to Ghana
Is the promise to be at peace with others
Because we are all Ghanian citizens
To fulfil the promise to Ghana
We must care for one another
And stop the violence in the land

Class Activities

1. Teacher: Find hard words in the story above and explain them to the students and further explain the effects on the nation if there is Coup d'etat in Ghana.
2. Teach them of the need to pray for menaces to change instead of feeling bad about thm.
3. Ask students of their views about the people that are considered menaces.
4. Tell them to memorize the poem or compose it into a song.

STORY SIXTEEN
And Loyal To Ghana

There were two girls called Faithful and Loyal. Though each came from the Upper West and Volta Regions of Ghana, they went to the same school in Brong Ahafo where they were taught about love of their motherland by loving one another, no matter where they come from.

Faithful grew up into a full time housewife of a rich man from the Eastern Region known as Chief while Loyal became a lawyer, living with her husband and her children in Upper West. Though they were far away from each other, they remained friends until Chief was poisoned by a menace in his family who wanted to take over his properties. The poison later killed him. This made Faithful and her children very sad. As they were crying over the dead, the menace went to tell other members of the family that it was Faithful who killed her husband so that she could inherit the properties.

The family believed the menace and sent Faithful and her children out of the house. When Loyal heard what happened, she left her own family in the North and went to the East to fight for her friend and sister.

They prayed together to God to help them fight the menace.

Loyal began to find out how and who poisoned Chief while at the same time she went to court to argue that the family has no right to sit over Chief's properties. She argued that Faithful and her children owned them.

Later the menace who poisoned Chief was discovered through the housemaid who said she saw him putting the poison in his drinks.

The menace was later handed over to the police and the properties were given back to Faithful.

Faithful wanted to give Loyal lots of money as a form of appreciation but she refused it, saying, "I didn't do it for money. I did it because you are my sister and friend. I also did it to fulfil the promise I made to Ghana. By fighting the battle with you, I am being faithful and loyal to my country."

Faithful with her children later took Loyal who had become their heroine to where she would take off to Upper West Region.

POEM: THE PROMISE TO BE LOYAL
The pledge to be loyal to God
Is to be the keeper of other people
The pledge to be loyal to Ghana
Is to support the goals of the nation,
fight against the vices in the land
And promote peace and unity

Class Activities

1. Teacher: Ask students what they learned in the story.
2. Let them know that through love and care for one and another, they can overcome menaces.
3. Find hard words in stories 15 and 16 and explain them.
4. Tell them to memorize the poem or compose it into a song.

STORY SEVENTEEN
My Motherland

The coastal water of the motherland of Ghana was once calm and peaceful as the fishes and their little ones went about their activities. Both old and young fishes were free to move up and down until some sharks invaded the sea, killing so many fishes for food.

There was a Mother Fish whose husband was killed by one of the sharks when going to look for food for the family. This gave Mother Fish the burden to look after their three little

ones Called Disobedience who was born first. Curious was the second while Obedience was the last child.

The little fishes lived in a small house called Safe Haven with their mother who always used her gift of mind to protect them from the sharks. She also always prayed to God to help her everyday as she went around the water to look for food and other things they would need in Safe Haven. As part of her duties, she taught the little ones how to trust in God; making them to follow all her instructions. She also warned them about the danger outside Safe Haven though she did not tell them about the sharks. She thought they might be frightened if they were told it was a shark that killed their father.

One day, Curious asked Mother Fish, 'why do we have to stay in Safe Haven?' She told them that when they grew older, they would understand.

Disobedience felt she was old enough to find out what was happening outside Safe Haven. She decided to go out to look for fun with other young fishes who also believed they were old enough to be on their own. As they were having fun, a young shark who pretended to be one of their friends told them to follow him to a funfair where they would enjoy themselves. When they got there, other sharks captured and ate them up as food.

Mother Fish now told the rest of her little ones more about the sharks. They did not disobey their mother until they grew up enough to find ways to drive the sharks out so that there may peace in the water of motherland.

Learn from the story of the little fishes and learn to follow instructions, rules and regulations in our motherland called Ghana.

POEM: LET THERE BE PEACE, GOD!

God Who created us we call on You
Let there be peace in our motherland
Make us to fear You in all our ways
So that we can be all law-abiding
Use us to put wrong things right
So that we can enjoy Your peace.

Class Activities

1. Teacher: Explain sharks in the story as those who threatens the peace of Ghana and how they cause trouble.
2. Ask them of the lessons in the story.
3. Tell them to memorize the poem or compose it into a song.

STORY EIGHTEEN
I Pledge Myself

Richard was the smallest boy in the class though he was not the youngest. His parents were so poor that they could hardly give him and their other children everything they need. This made him looked so weak and small.

All other students normally laughed at him. They would call him names like "Richard, the small boy" or "Richard, the weak boy." He could not play football like other boys. He could not answer any of the questions the teacher asked him in the class even if he knew the answer. He was always afraid that the rest would laugh at him if he tried to do anything. His mates maltreated him in the class. He thought he was not a normal child.

One day, his mother took him to a birthday party of her friend's son where he met many other children. Because he was made to feel bad about himself, he went to sit alone somewhere. A boy called Moses went to make friends with him. Soon they began to talk about many things. Richard told Moses how the students in the class treated him.

'If they treat you like that,' Moses said, 'you don't have to feel bad about yourself. Instead you must believe in God who created you the way you are! You must remember that you pledge yourself to be of service to Ghana. If you make this promise, you must believe in yourself that you can use your gifts to serve to your country. If you don't believe in yourself, you cannot be trained to be useful. You must also practice what you can do best until you become good enough to prove it to others that you are not weak.'

Richard became excited about what he learned from his new friend. From that day, he began to study hard. He also practiced how to run fast. When his mother sent him on an errand, he would run there as fast as he could. Guess what was the result of the study and the practice. He came third in the examination. During the school inter-house sport, he got a gold medal in relay race! Then many children in the class began to make friends with him, calling him new names: Richard, the brilliant boy or the medalist.

POEM: I AM MADE BY GOD

God who created Ghana created me
It does not matter what others say
I believe God gives me the things
Which I need before I can fulfill
The pledge I make to my country
I believe in what God made me to be
I'm wonder of the whole wide world!

Class Activities

1. Teacher: Ask what the students learned in the story above and point it to them that everybody has a gift.
2. Find hard words in story 17 and 18 and explain them.
3. Tell them to memorize the poem or compose them into a song.

STORY NINETEEN

To Service Of Ghana

Miss Benson was taught when she was getting trained as a school teacher that teaching people, especially young ones is a noble profession because it is one of the ways to build them into great Compatriots. She is made to believe that if she teaches the students the right way of life, she is fulfilling part of the promise she made to Ghana in the area of service. For these reasons, she loves teaching young ones in the School and in the Church. She would teach them about the word of God and how they could become great. She would say, "I have a dream. My dream is to make your dream come true. If you don't have a dream, I want to give you one. I want you to dream that you become a doctor or an engineer or a lawyer or a nurse or an accountant or a Minister of God. I will teach you all you need to know before you begin to realize your dream and I will tell you what you must not do if you want to become great."

Miss Benson would teach them many things in their books, including The Young Ghanian Story Book. She would give them home work and help them in the Class Activities. Soon, all the young ones start dreaming of becoming great in future, working so hard to fulfil their dreams and their promises.

One of the students

who was a girl went to Miss Benson one day and said, "I want to be greater than any of the students in the school."

"That's great!" Miss Benson said, looking excited. "I love that."

"I'll tell you the person I think is the greatest of all."

"Who?" Miss Benson asked quickly and curiously.

"I think you're the greatest," she said, making Miss Benson to look puzzled. "You're the giver of dreams. Without you, nobody will think of becoming great. And I would like to be just like you, the great giver of great dreams." Miss Benson felt so happy to hear this from her student that she hugged her.

Poem: I DON'T DAYDREAM BUT I HAVE A DREAM

I don't daydream to make money
Through dishonest manner
But I have a dream to be great
Through my service to Ghana
I will never dream to be comfortable
At the expense of fellow citizens
But I dream to be of help to them

Class Activities

1. Teacher: Find out the impact of the stories so far from the students by asking them about their dreams, including the ones for Ghana.
2. Explain the poem and ask them the reasons they must not make money through dishonest manner.
3. Make them memorize the poem or compose it into a song.

STORY TWENTY
With All My Strength And With All My Hearth

There were two mother monkeys, living on the mountains with their babies. There was fire outbreak one day. Every monkey living on the mountains began to shout: "There is fire on the mountain! Run! Run! Run!" Each mother monkey trapped her baby on her back and began to run as fast as she could, shouting like the rest: "There is fire on the mountain! Run! Run! Run!"

One of the mother monkeys was not careful enough. She stumbled over some woods and fell into the fire with the baby. The baby cried to his mother, "get up, Mama! Get up, Mama! We are going to die inside the fire if you don't get up!" But the mother monkey could not get up because she was wounded and tired of running.

The baby who had been taught to always trust in God and use all his strength and heart to serve motherland moved from her back. He got ready to get out of the fire. He knew he must also help his mother out of the fire otherwise she would die inside. As little he was, he tried to pull his mother away from the fire. But she was too heavy for him to lift or pull. Then he remembered the things he had been taught about God in the schools through the National Anthem that says: "God Bless Our Homeland Ghana And Make Our Nation Great And Strong, Bold To Defend Forever The Cause Of Freedom And Of Right; Fill Our Hearts With True Humanity, Make Us Cherish Fearless Honesty, And Help Us Resist Oppressor's Rule With All Our Will And Might For Evermore." Because he made the prayer in the Anthem, God gave him the strength to rescue himself, his mother and many others from the fire on the mountain.

The second mother monkey kept running without looking back to see what the little one was doing. Wherever the baby monkey saw people selling items like bananas and oranges, he would snatch them until everybody began to call the mother monkey a thief. You know why? They thought she taught her baby to be stealing those things. They stopped the mother monkey and beat her until she was wounded. Yes, she suffered for the wrong things baby monkey did.

If you want your parents to be proud of you, you must always do the right thing. If you do the wrong thing like stealing, nobody would be proud of you because soome people may suffer from it.

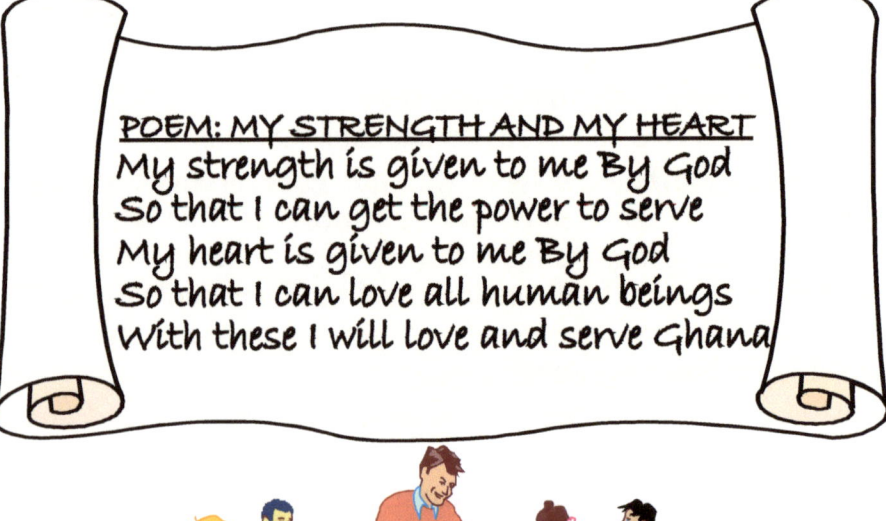

POEM: MY STRENGTH AND MY HEART
My strength is given to me By God
So that I can get the power to serve
My heart is given to me By God
So that I can love all human beings
With these I will love and serve Ghana

Class Activities

1. Teacher: Ask the students what they learned in the story.
2. Tell them to retell it to their parents and write down their responses.
3. Tell them to memorize the poem or compose it into a song.

STORY TWENTY-ONE
I Promise To Hold In High Esteem Our Heritage Won For Us

Martins learned so many good things at home and the in school, including how to fear God and abide by the rules and regulations through the National Anthem and The Pledge to Ghana. He was also made to promise to hold in high esteem the heritage of Ghana which is to stand by what he was taught as in the Culture, lessons in Civil Responsibilities and Moral Instruction Classes.

One day, two of the students went to him during the break time and said, "We're going out to look for fun! Would you like to go with us?"

"Where is the place?" Martins asked.

"You will know the place when we get there," they replied. And so Martins followed them without knowing where the naughty boys planned to go.

The place was a nearby orange farm. The students always went there to steal some of the oranges. When they got to the farm, they told Martins to watch and inform them if anyone was coming while they get busy plucking ripe oranges.

It was after the two boys have climbed the trees that Martins realized that they have come to steal oranges! He became very confused. He did not know what to do until got an idea.

Suddenly, he shouted at the boys, "someone is watching us!" Guess what happened. The boys jumped down from the trees and fled like birds.

Martins later went to join them in the school and told them, "you cannot run away from the person that is watching us."

The students asked him, "who is the person?"

Martins said, "it is God. He is everywhere, watching everything we all do even in secret. He blesses those who do the right thing and punishes anyone who does wrong thing."

It was then the boys remembered what they have been taught in school about God and upholding the heritage of Ghana by doing the right thing.

Poem: HERITAGE OF GHANA

Ghanaian heritage is beautiful
Because it is full of morals
It makes us very responsible
And makes us loyal people
I will hold in high esteem
The beautiful heritage of Ghana
Because I am a Ghanian!

Class Activities

1. Teacher: Ask the students what they learned in the story.
2. Find out hard words in Story 19 to 21 and explain them.
3. Make them memorize the poem or compose it into a song.

STORY TWENTY-TWO

Through The Blood And Toil Of Our Fathers

There was once a huge apple tree. A little boy loved to play around it everyday. He would climb the top of the tree, eat the apples and take a nap under it. The two of them loved each other very much.

As time went by, the little boy grew up. When he became a youth, he did not have time to play around the tree. One day, he went back to the tree with a sad look on his face. "Come and play with me," the tree told him.

"I'm no longer a kid. I cannot play around you anymore," the boy replied. "I want computer games instead. I need money to buy them."

"Sorry, I don't have money but you can pick all my apples and sell them. You can use the money to buy what you want."

The boy was excited as he grabbed all the apples on the tree and left happily. He did not come back after picking the apples. The tree was sad until the day he returned. The tree was happy and said, "let us play now."

"I don't have time to play. I have to go and work for the money to build a house for my family."

"I'm Sorry, I don't have a house but you can cut my branches and use them to build your house." The boy cut all the branches of the tree and left happily. The tree was glad to see him happy but he did not come back afterward. The tree felt lonely and sad again until the day he returned.

Feeling delighted, the tree said, "Come and play with me."

"I'm sad and too old for that," the man replied. "I want to go sailing and relax myself. Can you give me a boat?"

"You can cut down my trunk and build your boat with it. You can sail far away and be happy." The boy cut down the tree trunk to make a boat. He went sailing. He did not come back. He finally returned after many years.

"I'm sorry, son," the tree said sadly. "I don't have any more thing to give you. No more apples, no more branches and trunk except my dying root. I have given you the best of me just to make you happy." The man burst out in tears because he knew he was so selfish that he did not think of the comfort of the good old tree that gave him everything to make him happy.

He went to hug the tree and said, "please, forgive me for not giving you the love and care you really deserve for all you have done for me."

The tree represents parents and founding fathers of Ghana who sacrificed so much while the man is the citizen who is concerned only about himself.

POEM: I CANNOT ASK FOR MORE

Mum, Dad, I cannot ask for more
Not after all you did before now
Mum, you carry me in your womb
For nine months I feasted on you
Like a parasite in your big stomach
When I was born, I suck your milk
Each time I need some food to eat
You gave it to me without any complaint
Dad, I appreciate you for what you are
You are the bread winner and our shelter
You provide for everybody in the family
Come rain, come shine, you are always out
Looking for everything we need at home
I cannot ask you for more, Mum and Dad
Thank you for being there for me all the time

Class Activities

1. Teacher: Tell students some of the sacrifices of the founding fathers of Ghana.
2. Make them write an essay on the one whose life inspires or challenges them most.
3. Tell them to memorize the poem or compose it into a song.

STORY TWENTY-THREE
And I Pledge Myself In All Things

Before you read this story, you must note that just because adults are breaking the pledges they make to Ghana when they were young by doing the wrong thing does not make them right. The story is about you fulfilling your promises by doing what is right. It is also about correcting the wrong things which you might have learned in your environments or through your role models like parents or teachers.

Anita lived in Ashanti Region with her parents who were not rich but they could afford to get most of the things they need everyday.

Her mother was fond of borrowing things from the neighbour even though she knew she was supposed to buy those things in the market.

One day, Anita's aunty who was a school teacher in another town came to spend the weekend with them. The few days she spent proved that Anita who was in primary school was learning wrong things through her mother.

On one of the days, the aunty asked Anita whose mother went out on a visit, "where do you keep the matches? I need some in the kitchen."

"There is none in the house, aunty," Anita replied, "but my mother used to borrow some from the neighbours."

"Please, get it for me right away."

Anita went out to get it. She later returned with a full pack of matches.

When her aunty finished using it, she told her to return it. Anita said, "my mother used to take some of it and keep them before I return it. That is what she used to do even if she is given a bottle of oil or a sachet of salt."

Her aunty looked surprised and said, "that's stealing!"

"No," Anita said. "Mother does not steal. She told me she takes some of the items in case she needs them next time."

When Anita's mother returned home, the aunty told her she was teaching her little girl how to steal, telling her what happened.

Anita's mother decided to change her attitude for Anita's sake.

POEM: MY PLEDGE TO GHANA

I have made these pledges to Ghana:
I will be honest, faithful and loyal;
To serve the country with my heart
And my strength and gift of mind,
Holding in high esteem our heritage
I am determined to fulfill my pledge
Even if others fail in their promises
God will bless me and my country
As I fulfill my promises to Ghana!

Class Activities

1. Teacher: Ask the students what they learned in the story and find out wrong things they have seen adults doing and correct them.
2. Further explain the implication of breaking the law by breaking the pledge with the use of story 14
3. Help them memorize the poem or compose it into a song.

STORY TWENTY-FOUR
To Uphold And Defend

There is always tug of war going in every nation, including Ghana between Compatriots and menaces who always team up with mice to eat the cake the people laboured bakes. The Compatriots are doing all they can to preserve the cake for the people, including unborn children while the menaces and the mice are trying to eat it and destroy the things that are used to bake it.

The Compatriots know that menaces and mice will continue to increase if they are allowed to get away with the problems they always cause. So some of them become Lawyers who will bring the menaces and mice to justice and some join the police force who will arrest them and put them in prison. Some of them also become politicians and other leaders who would lead the country on the right part. While some other Compatriots become doctors who treat people when they are sick; some become teachers who teach young minds the right things; some engineers who build houses and other things; some become scientists who would invent things that would make life comfortable for the people and so many others do one thing or the other that serves as means to uphold and defend the nation of Ghana.

Young Compatriot like you must understand that the behaviours of citizens are the real riches of the nation. What that means is that if a country has no natural resources like gold, oil and other things but has Compatriots who are ready to build the nation with their strengths; hearts and gifts of mind, it would become rich; peaceful and successful. On the other hand, if the country is rich with natural resources that can bring money but the motherland is filled with mice and menaces, they would destroy these things and make the people to suffer hunger in the midst of plenty food. You must learn to defend Ghana against mice and menaces.

POEM: TO UPHOLD AND DEFEND GHANA
To learn how to uphold Ghana
I must always learn from my teachers
And study my books so that I can pass
Instead of cheating during examination
To learn how to defend Ghana
I must tell others to be of good behaviour
Instead of joining the young menaces

Class Activities

1. Teacher: Review all the stories about menaces and mice and tell the students to compare their natures with Compatriots'.
2. Find hard words in story 22 to 24 and explain them.
3. Tell them to memorize the poem or compose it into a song.

STORY TWENTY-FIVE
The Good Name Of Ghana

John was taught how to uphold and defend the good name of Ghana and his family by doing and saying the right things at home and in the school. He chose to be a stubborn and unruly boy until the day his mother made some spaghetti for the family to have as dinner. She had also fried some chicken and kept it in the fridge for the next day. John who hated to eat spaghetti said, 'mum, I want rice and fried chicken.'

His mother told him to go to bed hungry if he did not want spaghetti.

Angrily, John went to bed but he could not sleep because he felt hungry.

After everybody has gone to bed, he sneaked into the kitchen to take part of the fried chicken in the fridge.

He sat beside the fridge in the dark, eating the chicken in the kitchen.

When his mother heard noises in the kitchen, she went to the place to find out what was there. She asked in a low voice, 'who is there?'

Of course, John kept silent. He thought she would soon go away. When she did not go, he grunted and made noises like a wild animal.

His mother ran out of the place and went to his father who was sleeping. She woke him up and said, 'there is a wild animal in the kitchen!'

His father quickly stood up from the bed and went to the place.

John heard their footsteps as he was still enjoying the stolen chicken. He made another wild noises though he was still chewing the meat.

His mother ran again but his father did not. He took a long

stick of a mop that was closed to him and walked quietly to the side of the fridge where the noise came from. Because it was too dark to see, he did not know it was John sitting down, eating his mother's chicken. He struck him on the head.

John fell down on the ground, opening his mouth as if he was dead. The chicken fell out of his mouth.

His father said to his mother, 'I've killed the animal bring the light.'

When she brought the light, they discovered that it was John. He was unconscious. Looking surprised to see him, they took him into the hospital at once. He later woke up the following day with heavy bandage on his head. It was then he understood the reason he must always do the right thing all the time. He dared not steal again

TO UPHOLD THE GOOD NAME OF GHANA

To uphold the good name of Ghana
I will never cheat during examination
To uphold to uphold the name of my family
I will be honest in everything I do
To uphold the name of my community
I will not eat rotten meat of the vultures

Class Activities

1. Teacher: Ask students what te learn in the story.
2. Ask students the ways they can uphold and defend the good name of Ghana.
3. Tell them to memorize the poem or compose it into a song.
4. Ask students who are gifted in drama to dramatize the story.

STORY TWENTY-SIX
So Help Me God.

There were twin sisters who lived with their aged grandmother. Granny as she was called by the twin sisters strongly believed in God. She took care of them and taught them about faith and trust in God.

They have a farmland where they planted crops for sale and for food. God always brought them great harvest in the farm by giving them rain. Because she knew it was God that provided for them, Grammy also taught the twin sisters of the need to share their things with needy people.

There was a time when rain did not fall. This caused famine in the land. Because of this, there was lack of food and money to buy all they needed.

The twin sisters and Granny felt the famine so much that they always prayed that God should continue to feed them.

One day, Granny felt like eating some bread but there was no money to buy it. The twin sisters and Granny decided to pray about it in the sitting room, saying, "Oh, God, you have always provided for us. Please, give us some loaves of bread and some butter."

Some naughty boys who did not believe there is God heard them praying. They said among themselves, "let us give them some bread and butter. It will make them feel it is God who gives them. When they finish eating, we will go and tell them we gave them and not God because there is no God."

"That is a brilliant idea. It will make feel like fools for believing in God."

They contributed some money and went to buy loaves of

bread and a tin of butter. They threw them inside the sitting room through the window.

The twins and Granny were happy when they saw them. They thanked God for the food, eating some of the bread and butter.

As they finished eating, the boys came into the house to tell them they were the ones that gave them the loaves of bread and butter, not God.

One of the sisters argued, "It is God who gave us when we prayed."

"We threw the bread and butter inside when we heard your prayers."

Granny said, "God gave them to us even if he used little devils to give us."

TO UPHOLD AND DEFEND THE GOOD NAME OF GHANA
To uphold the good name of Ghana
I will never take what is not mine
And I will never tell any lie
To defend the good name of Ghana
I will always do the right thing
To defend the nation against enemies
I will fight against menaces and mice
God will help me for I am a Compatriot!

Class Activities

(1) Teacher: Find hard words in story 25 to 26 and explain them.
(2) Tell students to review titles of all the stories together, reciting them as The National Anthem and The Pledge Th Ghana.
(3) Tell them to memorize the poem or compose it into a song.

1ST SERIES OF WEEKLY GHANIAN CHILDREN AND YOUTH ORIENTATION STUDIES

1ST STANZA OF THE ANTHEM: LINES 1 TO 8

TEACHER: *Note that this manual is designed to be used on school assembly ground within 10 minutes with the stories in this book. The book is also used as civics, moral and other textbooks in classrooms.*

Week 1: Read Story One With The Title:

Line 1: GOD BLESS OUR HOMELAND, GHANA
Line 2: AND MAKE OUR NATION GREAT AND STRONG,

A. Line 1 begins with requests or prayers to God to protect, make good and be with Ghana which is the home of all Ghanaians.
B. Line 2 also requests God to make the nation very good or pleasant and powerful.
C. When you say lines 1 and 2, you actually pray to God to protect and to be with Ghana which is the home of all Ghanaians and also to make it very good, pleasant and powerful.

Memorize This: I will always pray for Ghana, my country, so that it can be well with everybody.

Week 2: Read Story Two With The Title:

Line 3: BOLD TO DEFEND FOREVER
Line 4: THE CAUSE OF FREEDOM AND OF RIGHT,

A. Line 3 prays to God to use laws in Ghana and make the leaders able or courageous enough to protect the nation as long as it exists.
B. Line 4 continues the prayer to protect what belongs to citizens and make them free from problems and enemies of the nation.
C. When you say lines 3 and 4, you pray to God to make use of the laws and leaders in Ghana to protect what belongs to citizens and make them free from problems and enemies of the nation.

Memorize This: I pray that God will give Ghana good leaders who will uphold the law, protect the citizens and make them free from problems.

Week 3: Read Story Three With The Title:

Line 5: FILL OUR HEARTS WITH TRUE HUMANITY,
Line 6: MAKE US CHERISH FEARLESS HONESTY,

A. Line 5 prays to God to give all Ghanaians the feelings of love with care for one another.
B. Line 6 prays that God makes them understand the need to be truthful without fear of anything.
C. When you say lines 5 and 6, you pray to God to make you love and care for other citizens and to make you able to tell the truth without fear.

Memorize This: I pray to God to make me love others as I love myself and to make me truthful in all my ways.

Week 4 Read Story Four The Title:

Line 7: AND HELP US RESIST OPPRESSOR'S RULE
Line 8: WITH ALL OUR WILL AND MIGHT FOR EVERMORE

A. Line 7 prays to God to help citizens stop from ruling Ghana anyone who would make people suffer.
B. Line 8 means that with the minds and powers, including talents of citizens as long as they live.
C. When you say lines 7 and 8, you pray to God to help you to stop from ruling Ghana anyone who will make the citizens to suffer, using your mind and with what God has given to you as powers; including your talents and wisdom as long as you live.

Memorize This: I pray to God to give me the ability and the wisdom to defend my country against anyone who wants to ruin it.

TEACHER: Recall all the titles of the four stories and tell the students to sing them as 1st Stanza of the National Anthem. Since repetition is required in thorough orientation, all the lessons are to be repeated through out the remaining weeks in the term. The 2nd stanza will be studied next term. During the studies, there is need to ask them questions and tell them to recite the memorized portion.

2ND SERIES OF WEEKLY GHANAIAN CHILDREN AND YOUTH ORIENTATION STUDIES

2ND STANZA OF THE ANTHEM: LINES 1 TO 8

TEACHER: *Note that this manual is designed to be used on school assembly ground within 10 minutes with the stories in this book. The book is also used as civics, moral and other textbooks in classrooms.*

Week 1: Read Story Five With The Title:

Line 1: HAIL TO THY NAME, O GHANA
Line 2: TO THEE WE MAKE OUR SOLEMN VOW;
Line 3: STEADFAST TO BUILD TOGETHER

A. Line 1 calls your attention to the name of Ghana, making you to see it as a very good thing.
B. Line 2 makes all citizens to make important promises to the nation.
C. Line 3 makes you promise that you will help in making the nation to develop or to progress.
D. When you say lines 1 to 3, you call the name of Ghana with respect and promise that you will help in developing or in making the nation to progress or advance in every area you can help or support.

Memorize This: I will always go to school and study my books so that I can be useful and productive to my country, Ghana.

Week 2: Week 1: Read Story Six With The Title:

Line 4: A NATION STRONG IN UNITY;
Line 5: WITH OUR GIFTS OF MIND AND STRENGTH OF ARM,

A. Line 4 makes all citizens to promise that they would come together as one and make Ghana so powerful that nothing can make it weak.
B. Line 5 makes all citizens to promise that they will make the nation strong with the use of the gifts like wisdom and talents, which God has given them, also using other things like police force to protect the nation against others or people who cause problems or who break the law.
C. When you say lines 4 and 5, you actually promise that you will join others in using the talents God gives to you and the forces of Ghana to make the nation very powerful.

Memorize This: I promise to make my country, Ghana, proud with the use of my talents.

Week 3: Read Story Seven With The Title:

Line 6: WHETHER NIGHT AND DAY, IN MIDST OF STORM,

A. "Whether night and day" means the promise to be of help to the nation and other citizens in times of needs at anytime of the day and night.
B. "In midst of storm" means the promise to be of help to the nation even when it is difficult.
C. When you say lines 6, you actually promise to be of help to the nation and other citizens in times of needs at anytime of the day and night even when if it is difficult to be of help.

Memorize This: I will always do my best to be of help to the nation and my fellow citizens.

Week 4 Read Story Eight With The Title:

Line 7: IN EVERY NEED WHATE'ER THE CALL MAY BE,
Line 8: TO SERVE THEE, GHANA, NOW AND EVERMORE

A. Line 7 makes all Ghanaians to promise to do all they can to be of help in every area the nation needs them such as protecting children against danger.
B. Line 8 continues the promise to answer the call to serve the nation such as helping those who are involved motor accidents.
C. When you say lines 7 and 8, you actually promise the nation to be of help in every area you are needed, answering the call of other citizens who are in need of your help as long as you live.

Memorize This: I will always help those who need my help so that God can also use others to help me whenever I need their help.

TEACHER: Recall all the titles of the eight stories in the two terms and tell the students to sing them as 1st and 2nd stanzas of the National Anthem. Since repetition is required in orientation, all the lessons are to be repeated through out the remaining weeks in the term. The 3rd stanza will be studied next term.

3RD SERIES OF WEEKLY GHANIAN CHILDREN AND YOUTH ORIENTATION STUDIES
3RD STANZA OF THE ANTHEM: LINES 1 TO 8

TEACHER: *Note that this manual is designed to be used on the assembly ground within 10 minutes.*

Week 1: Read Story Nine Of The Book With The Title:

Line 1: RAISE HIGH THE FLAG OF GHANA
Line 2: AND ONE WITH AFRICA ADVANCE;

A. Line 1 tells all citizens to always make others know that they are proud of Ghana through the display of the flag which is one of the things that show what the nation stands for.
B. Line 2 makes all Ghanaians believe in the unity of Africa and be united with other Africans in moving the continent forward in areas like economy and social welfare.
C. When you say lines 1 and 2, you tell yourself to be proud of Ghana and join other Africans to move the continent forward.

Memorize This: I am proud to be a citizen of Ghana who will join other Africans to make Africa a great continent.

Week 2: Read Story Ten Of The Book With The Title:

Line 3: BLACK STAR OF HOPE AND HONOUR
Line 4: TO ALL WHO THIRST FOR LIBERTY;

A. Line 3 makes all Ghanaians to see themselves as black people and as stars who give hope and bring deep respect to others.
B. Line 4 makes citizens to believe in themselves as black people who bring hope and respect to other nations that want to be free like Ghana.
C. When you say lines 3 and 4, you tell yourself that you are the black person who is the star that brings hope and respect to other people who want to be free.

Memorize This: I am wonderfully made by God so that I can give hope and joy to other people.

Week 3: Read Story Eleven Of The Book With The Title:

Line 5: WHERE THE BANNER OF GHANA FREELY FLIES,

A. "Where the banner of Ghana" means (i) anywhere the flag is flown (ii) wherever and whenever the National Anthem and (iii) The Pledge To Ghana are recited.
B. "Freely flies" means to be ready to follow what the Anthem and The Pledge say before you are free to claim your right as a citizen of Ghana.
C. When you say line 5, you tell yourself of the need to follow what the National Anthem says, fulfill the pledge you make to Ghana before you can be free to claim your right as a citizen.

Memorize This: Since the National Anthem is part of the law and The Pledge is what I must fulfill, I will follow them as a reasonable and responsible citizen of Ghana.

Week 4 Read Story Twelve Of The Book With The Title:

Line 6: MAY THE WAY TO FREEDOM TRULY LIE;

A. "May the way" means by doing what the Anthem says and fulfilling the pledge, you follow the way.
B. "Of freedom truly lie" means where you can really find freedom.
C. When you say lines 6, you say that when you follow what the anthem says and fulfill the pledge you make to Ghana, you actually follow the true way to freedom.

Memorize This: I must be faithful, honest and loyal to my country so as to keep my freedom.

Week 5 Read Story Thirteen Of The Book With The Title:

Line 7: ARISE, ARISE, O SONS OF GHANA LAND
Line 8: AND UNDER GOD MARCH ON FOR EVERMORE!

A. Line 7 calls on all citizens of Ghana to get up or get ready to do all they are instructed to do in the anthem.
B. Line 8 means that with God leading everybody in the nation, the citizens must begin to move as long as Ghana exists.
C. When you say lines 7 and 8, you are actually instructed by the nation to get ready to help the nation to make progress with God leading the country.

Memorize This: With my faith in God and with the spirit of unity with others, I and my fellow citizens would move Ghana forward.

TEACHER: Recall all the titles of the twelve stories in the three terms and tell the students to sing them as 1st, 2nd and 3rd stanzas of the National Anthem.

4TH SERIES OF WEEKLY GHANAIAN CHILDREN AND YOUTH ORIENTATION STUDIES
PART ONE OF STUDIES OF "THE PLEDGE TO GHANA": LINES 1 TO 4

TEACHER: *Note that this manual is designed to be used on school assembly ground within 10 minutes with the stories in this book.*

Week 1: Read Story Fourteen Of The Book With The Title:
Line 1: I PROMISE, ON MY HONOUR
A. "I promise" means you vow or pledge to do everything you are going to say.
B. "On my honour" means with due respect to yourself.
C. When you say line 1, you actually vow or pledge to Ghana that, with due respect to yourself, you will do everything you are about to say.
   Memorize This: With God as my Witness and Helper, I am bound and committed to fulfill the promise I am making to my country, Ghana.

Week 2: Read Story Fifteen Of The Book With The Title: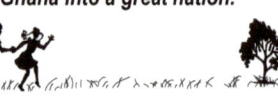
Line 2 (a) : TO BE FAITHFUL
A. "To be faithful" means to do what you agree to do, including being honest and truthful.
B. It also means to always help Ghana to develop in every area.
C. When you say "to be faithful", you actually promise to do everything you agree to do and help the nation to develop in every area of life.
   Memorize This: I am willing and able to support in building Ghana into a great nation.

Week 3: Read Story Sixteen Of The Book With The Title:
Line 2 (b) : AND LOYAL TO GHANA
A. "To be loyal to Ghana" means you will continue to be faithful to the nation without ceasing to do what you promise to do.
B. It also means that you will continue to be truthful and honest in the way you serve Ghana.
C. When you say "to be faithful and loyal to Ghana" in line 2, you promise to do everything you agree to do as in The National Anthem and The Pledge To Ghana, supporting the nation in every area of life without getting tired; including helping your fellow citizens who may be in need of you.
Memorize This: I will always serve Ghana by helping fellow Ghanaians who are in need of my help. So help me, God.

Week 4 Read Story Seventeen Of The Book With The Title:
Line 3: MY MOTHERLAND
A. "Mother" is the woman who gives to a person.
B. "Land" means a place or area.
C. When you say "My motherland" in line 3, you describe Ghana as a place that belongs to the woman who gives birth to you, saying that you will be faithful and loyal to the nation you come from.
   Memorize This: Come what may on my way on any day, I will never let down Ghana, my motherland.

Week 5 Read Story Eighteen Of The Book With The Title:
Line 4 (a): I PLEDGE MYSELF
A. "Pledge" means to vow or make promise to do something.
B. "Pledge myself" means to make yourself to make a vow or promise.
C. When you say "I pledge myself", you are making yourself to make a vow or promise to do something that is really important to do.
   Memorize This: I pray to God of all creations to help me fulfil the pledge I make to Ghana.

Week 6 Read Story Nineteen Of The Book With The Title:
Line 4 (b): TO SERVICE OF GHANA
A. "To the service of Ghana" means to be useful and helpful to Ghana.
B. It also means to be useful and helpful to other citizens of Ghana because you serve the nation by serving the people.
C. When you say line 4 (a and b), you make yourself to promise to be helpful and useful to the nation by helping other citizens.
   Memorize This: I also pray to God to make me useful and helpful to Ghana and fellow citizens.

TEACHER: Recall all the titles of the six stories. The rest of the lines in "The Pledge To Ghana" will be studied next term.

5TH SERIES OF WEEKLY GHANAIAN CHILDREN AND YOUTH ORIENTATION STUDIES

PART TWO OF STUDIES OF "THE PLEDGE TO GHANA": LINES 5 TO 14

TEACHER: *Note that this manual is designed to be used on school assembly ground within 10 minutes with the stories in this book. The book is also used as civics, moral and other textbooks in classrooms.*

Week 1: Read Story Twenty Of The Book With The Title:
Line 5: WITH ALL MY STRENGTH
Line 6: AND WITH ALL MY HEART
A. Line 5 means you promise to use all your abilities or powers to serve Ghana, including using your gift for the good of the nation.
B. Line 6 means you promise to put your mind to the service of Ghana.
C. When you say lines 5 and 6, you promise to use all your abilities and gifts to serve Ghana, putting your mind on the service.

Memorize This: The service to my country is noble. So I will service Ghana with love.

Week 2: Read Story Twenty-One Of The Book With The Title:
Line 7: I PROMISE TO HOLD IN HIGH ESTEEM
Line 8: OUR HERITAGE, WON FOR US
A. Line 7 means you vow to love and give lots of respect.
B. Line 8 means the good things like cultures, independence and freedom which the nation was able to get through struggles and battles.
C. When you say line 7 and 8, you pledge to Ghana to love and give lots of respect to the good things like cultures and independence or freedom that are made possible through struggles and battles other citizens.

Memorize This: I will love and respect the freedom of Ghana by obeying the law.

Week 3: Read Story Twenty-Two Of The Book With The Title:
Line 9: THROUGH THE BLOOD AND TOIL
Line 10: OF OUR FATHERS
A. Line 9 means the blood that was shed and the struggles of those who made it possible for Ghana to get freedom or independence.
B. Line 10 means people like the nationalists who fought and struggled for the freedom of Ghana.
C. When you say lines 9 and 10, you vow to love and respect the freedom of Ghana that was made possible by nationalists and other people.

Memorize This: I will always struggle to keep the freedom of Ghana by fighting against vices.

Week 4: Read Story Twenty-Three Of The Book With The Title:
Line 11: AND I PLEDGE MYSELF IN ALL THINGS
A. "I pledge myself" means that you make yourself promise.
B. "In all things" means in everything you do and say.
C. When you say line 11, you promise to Ghana that, in everything you do and say, you will do what is in the next line.

Memorize This: I will always do the right thing.

Week 5: Read Story Twenty-Four Of The Book With The Title:
Line 12: TO UPHOLD AND DEFEND

A. "To uphold" means to give support and do everything to lift something up.
B. "And defend" means to protect or prevent from danger or attack.
C. When you say line 12, you promise Ghana that you will do everything you can to support, lift up and prevent the nation from danger or attack.

Memorize This: Help me, God, to be one of the citizens who will uphold and defend Ghana, my country.

Week 6: Read Story Twenty-Five Of The Book With The Title:
Line 13: THE GOOD NAME OF GHANA:

A. "Good name" means all the good things that are known with someone.
B. "The good name of Ghana" means all the good things that are known with Ghana such as the things you have learnt in the National Anthem and The Pledge.
C. When you say line 13, you promise Ghana that you will support the good things that are known with Ghana and prevent it from attack or danger.

Memorize This: I am willing and able to support in building Ghana into a great nation.

Week 7: Read Story Twenty-Six Of The Book With The Title:

Line 14: SO HELP ME GOD

A. God is the Creator or the One Who creates everything and everyone in the world.
B. Because God is the Creator, He has the power to control everything and everyone.
C. When you say line 14, you actually pray to God to help you fulfil the promises you make to Ghana.

Memorize This: God, the Creator of all things will help me fulfil all the promises I make to Ghana.

TEACHER: First recall all the titles in Story 14 to 26 and make students recite The Pledge To Ghana. Then make them sing all the stanzas of the National Anthem. You can do the revisions of all the lessons from the beginning to the end for the rest of the term. While recalling the lessons, there is need to ask them questions and tell them to recite the memorized portion.

www.ingramcontent.com/pod-product-compliance
Lightning Source LLC
Chambersburg PA
CBHW042132080426
42735CB00005B/150